To Catch the Moon

Originally published in the Netherlands by Elzenga, Tilburg. The title of the Dutch edition is *Maantjelief*. Translated from the Dutch by Greta Kilburn.

All inquiries should be addressed to:
Barron's Educational Series, Inc.
250 Wireless Boulevard
Hauppauge, NY 11788

Library of Congress Catalog Card No.

International Standard Book No. 0–8120–6341–4 (hardcover)
0–8120–1559–2 (paperback)

Library of Congress Catalog Card No. 92-43067

Library of Congress Cataloging-in-Publication Data

Akkerman, Dinie.
[Maantjelief. English]
To catch the moon / concept and illustrations,
Dinie Akkerman;
text, Paul van Loon.
p.   cm.
Summary: Oscar the elephant and his friends fly to the
moon on a kite, but Oscar's weight causes the moon to
fall back to earth.
ISBN 0-8120-6341-4—ISBN 0-8120-1559-2 (pbk.)
[1. Moon—Fiction. 2. Elephants—Fiction.]
I. Loon, Paul van. II. Title.
PZ7.A3127To   1993
[E]—dc20
92-37700
CIP
AC

PRINTED IN CHINA
34567   4900   987654321

To Catch the Moon

Concept and Illustrations:
Dinie Akkerman

Text:
Paul van Loon

Translation:
Greta Kilburn

One evening, Oscar the Elephant was up and about with a pair of scissors, a jar of glue, and other important materials.

"What are you doing?" Paco asked.

"I'm making a kite," Oscar explained. "A moon kite. I am going to fetch my friend the moon with it. I've asked him to come and visit us."

"Do you think the kite will work?" asked Sara.

"Of course," replied Oscar. "You watch."

Oscar left the house with the kite under his arm.
"I hope it's going to be all right," thought Sara.

The elephant walked confidently down to the beach.
"It's a beautiful evening to fly a moon kite!" he exclaimed.
"How surprised everyone will be when I return with the moon."

Oscar started to run down the beach, with the kite trailing on the string behind him.

"Dear little moon, I'm on my way!" he cried.

But the kite only rose a short way and then dipped down again.

Oscar was getting worn-out.

Sara and Paco came out of the house. Oscar was sitting down, sadly staring into space.
"You see," said Sara, "it's not working. We'll have to help him, Paco."

Oscar happily jumped to his feet. He had almost lost hope.

"If you two help me, it's got to work," he said.

The three of them took hold of the kite string and ran down the beach.

The little animals in the dunes looked on with curiosity.

"Faster!" cried Oscar.

They ran and they ran and the kite rose a little way into the air.

"Faster still!"

Just then the wind slipped under the kite.

The kite shot up into the air and pulled Oscar, Sara, and Paco up with it. "Hang on tight," cried Oscar. "We are on our way to the moon!"

He gazed up happily, but Sara and Paco anxiously clung to the kite string. They rose higher and higher. Then, suddenly, the kite was no longer pulling them up. The wind had died down. The kite was crashing! Oscar, Sara, and Paco fell . . . on top of a cloud.

The cloud gently floated upward.
"We'll get there this way too," Oscar cried happily.
Sara and Paco said nothing. They had had a bit of a scare.

After a while they saw the moon ahead of them—big and yellow
like a banana. He looked very friendly.
"Ah, so we have arrived at last," said Oscar.

Paco was the first to step on the moon, followed by Sara.
But Oscar is fat and heavy. The moment he put one leg
on the moon it started to sink.
"That's just what we need," said Oscar.
"This way the moon will come home with us."

The way down seemed much faster than the way up. They whizzed like an arrow past stars and clouds.
Before they knew it, they plunged into the ocean.

"Help, we're going to drown!" cried Sara.

But the moon bobbed on the water like a beautiful yellow boat.

"What a good thing I still have my kite," said Oscar. "We couldn't wish for a better sail."

They sailed home with the wind filling the kite.

A wave threw the moon, Oscar, Sara, and Paco onto the beach.
Everything was still the same there: the house and the palm trees,
even the stars in the sky were still in the same place.
Except, the moon no longer was suspended among the stars. He was
lying a bit helplessly on the beach.

Oscar, Sara, and Paco picked up the moon. They carefully carried him over to Oscar's house.

"The sky looks empty without moonlight," said Sara.

But Oscar felt that it wasn't all that bad.

"There are plenty of stars, aren't there?" he reasoned.

Once they were home, they immediately got into bed.
"There is nothing as tiring as a trip to the moon," said Oscar.
"Especially when three leave and you come back with
a fourth!"
Paco and Sara soon fell asleep. But Oscar couldn't get to sleep. He peeped
through his eyelids at the moon, hanging right in front of his window.

The following day, Oscar, Sara, and Paco were awakened by voices outside their room.

Oscar instantly saw that the moon was no longer hanging in front of the window.

"The moon is gone," Oscar thought as he leapt out of bed.

But when they looked out of the window, they saw the moon lying on the ground. He looked very peculiar—ill and pale, as if all his color had left.

"Dear little moon, what's the trouble?" asked Oscar anxiously.

Fortunately, Doctor Rabbit was nearby.

He examined the moon and shook his head. "This is very bad," he said.

"A serious case of sunstroke."

"Oh, no!" exclaimed Oscar. "There is nothing wrong with my moon."

"The patient is absolutely unable to cope with sunlight," said the doctor.

"See that he gets plenty of shade. And when the sun has gone down, you must immediately send him back to where he came from."

"What are we waiting for?" cried Oscar. "Let's all get started!"

Help arrived from all sides. Poles, ropes, canvas, and blankets were
brought quickly. Everybody did his very best to protect the moon from
the sun.

Oscar worked hardest of all. "Keep it up, my dear little moon," he coaxed.

At last the sun disappeared behind the ocean. The moon got a bit
of color again.
Oscar quickly climbed a stepladder and tied the moon kite to the tip
of the moon.
"There's no time to lose," he urged. "We have to fly him at once."
"We'll help you," Sara and Paco offered.

Oscar sucked his cheeks full of air. Then he blew into the kite with all his might.

And, yes . . . The kite slowly started rising. It pulled the moon along—
higher, still higher, to the stars.
And the closer the moon came to the stars, the more he began to beam.

Oscar, Paco, and Sara sat on the beach. They looked at the moon and
thought of everything that had happened.
"Do you know . . ." said Oscar, "now I understand. The moon belongs up
there and we belong down here. And to tell you the truth, I think
he is even more beautiful up there than he was down here."

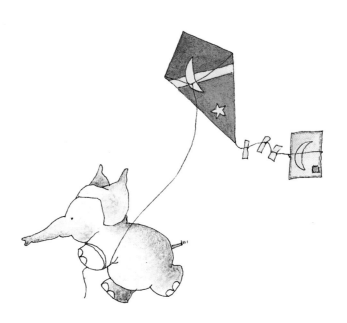